Sugarbug Doug

All About Cavities, Plaque and Teeth

by Dr. Ben Magleby

Summary: Sugarbug Doug (i.e. streptococcus mutans) is bacteria that lives in your mouth and causes tooth decay and gum disease. Learn how bacteria do this and how you can stop them from destroying your teeth.

Illustrations were hand drawn with ink and colored digitally.

For additional information and free educational downloads, please visit

www.sugarbugdoug.com

Copyright © 2008 Benjamin Magleby DDS
All rights reserved.
ISBN: 1-4392-2500-1
ISBN-13: 9781439225004
Library of Congress Control Number: 2009900215

Printed by CreateSpace,
an Amazon.com Company

For Heather

...and everyone else who doesn't like to go to the dentist.

This is Doug.
Doug is a sugarbug.
Even though he is very small,
Doug can still hurt you.

Because Doug is so small,
he can hide between your teeth.
He likes to hide there with
all his friends.

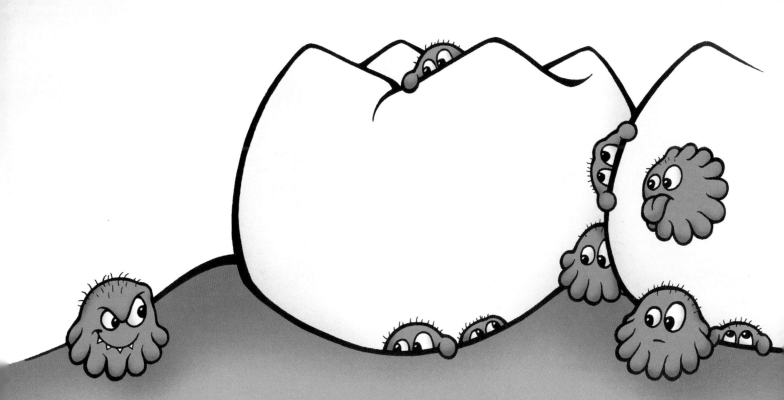

Doug loves his home.
He loves all of the food that he
finds stuck between your teeth.

Whenever Doug finds food,
he invites all his friends to
eat with him.

Not only does Doug eat your food,
he can also build a house out of it.
Doug feels safe in his house.

If Doug's house stays in your mouth for a long time, then sugarbugs can make his house bigger and stronger. Millions and millions of sugarbugs can live there.

Even though Doug's house is very small,
you can usually see it next to your gums,
or scrape it off with your fingernail.
Doug's house is called
plaque.

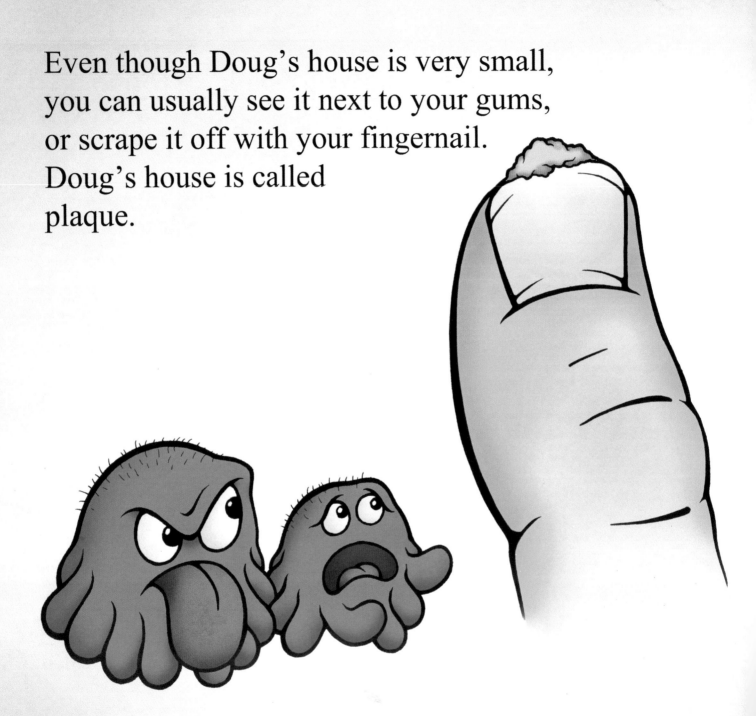

When Doug's house stays in your mouth for a long time, it gets much harder to scrape off. These stronger houses are called calculus or tartar.

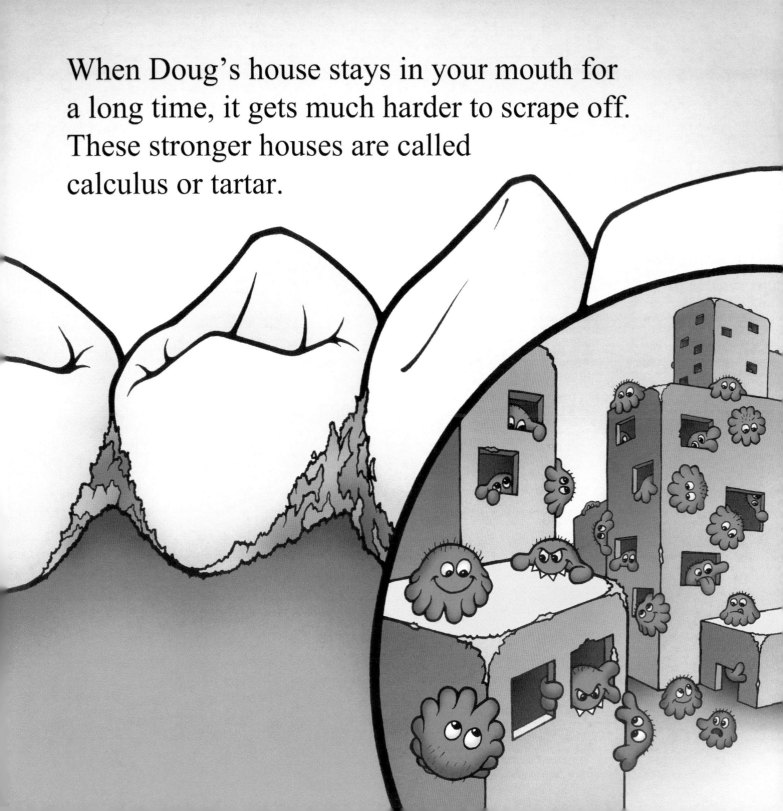

Doug's favorite food is sugar. There are many
different kinds of food that have sugar.

One of Doug's favorite drinks is soda pop.
Not only is most soda pop filled with sugar,
all soda pop has acid. All sugarbugs love acid.

Whenever Doug eats sugar,
he can make his own acid.
He likes to squirt his acid
on teeth.

When acid stays on your
teeth for a long time,
it makes them rot.
These rotten holes are
called cavities.

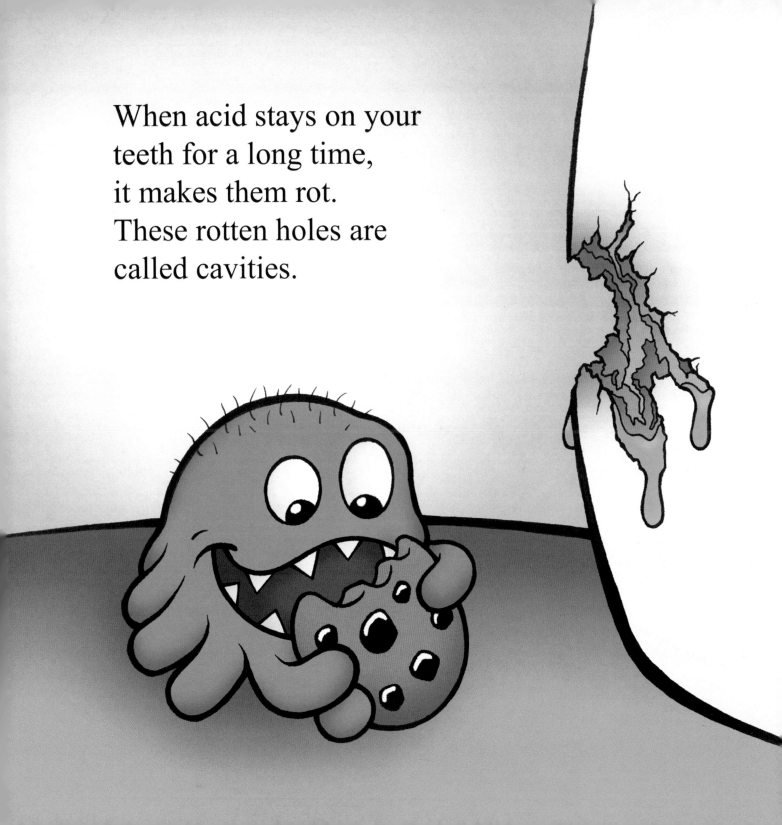

Doug can hide from the toothbrush in cavities. He feels safe there.

Sugarbugs can make cavities bigger and bigger. They can also move to your next tooth and start a cavity there too.

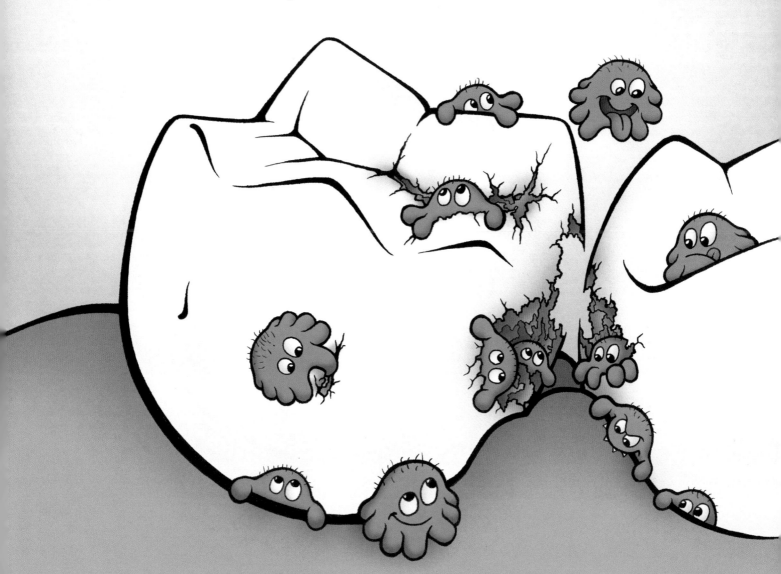

There are some foods that Doug doesn't like. Some of these are fresh vegetables, fruits and foods filled with protein, like cheese and nuts. Sugarbugs can't make as much acid from these foods.

Sugarless gum doesn't have the sugar that Doug likes. It cleans your teeth and takes away Doug's food. Sugarbugs can't stand gum like this!

Doug would much rather have some cookies or candy.

Doug doesn't like water because it washes away his food. What sugarbugs really hate is water with fluoride!

Fluoride from water or toothpaste makes
your teeth so strong that Doug's acid
can't make holes
in your teeth.

If a sugarbug
accidently eats
some fluoride,
it will kill him.

I'm dead!

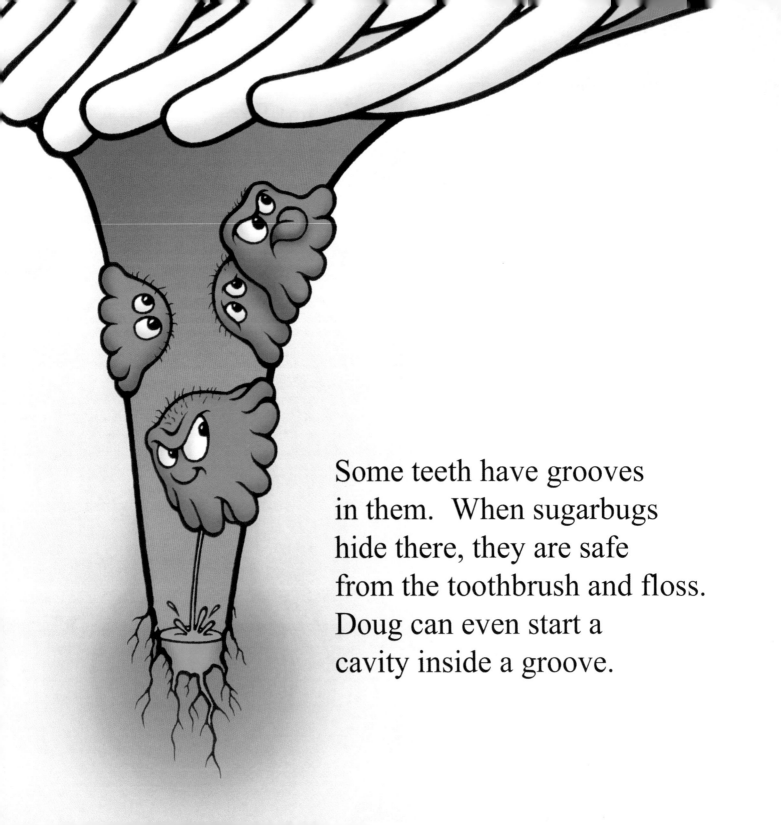

Some teeth have grooves in them. When sugarbugs hide there, they are safe from the toothbrush and floss. Doug can even start a cavity inside a groove.

A dentist can fill these grooves with plastic.
This is called a sealant. Doug doesn't like sealants!
He can't hide or start a cavity there,
he has to run away and hide somewhere else.

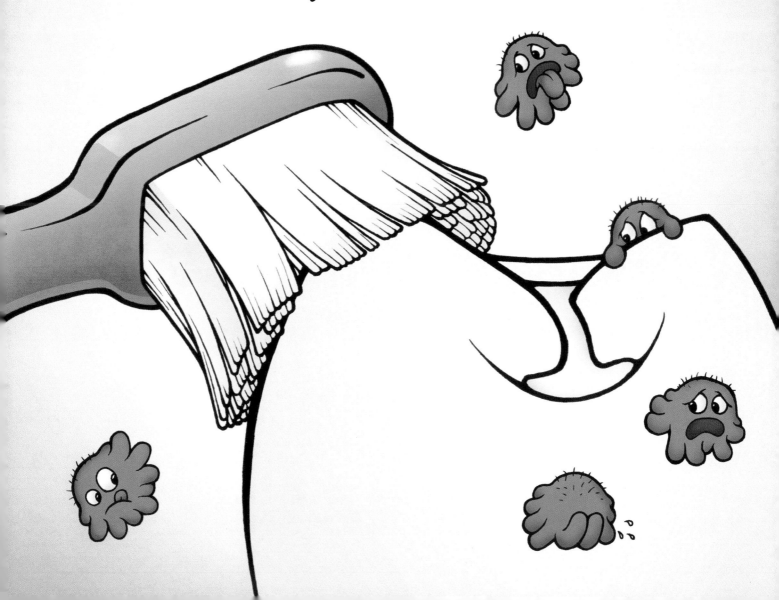

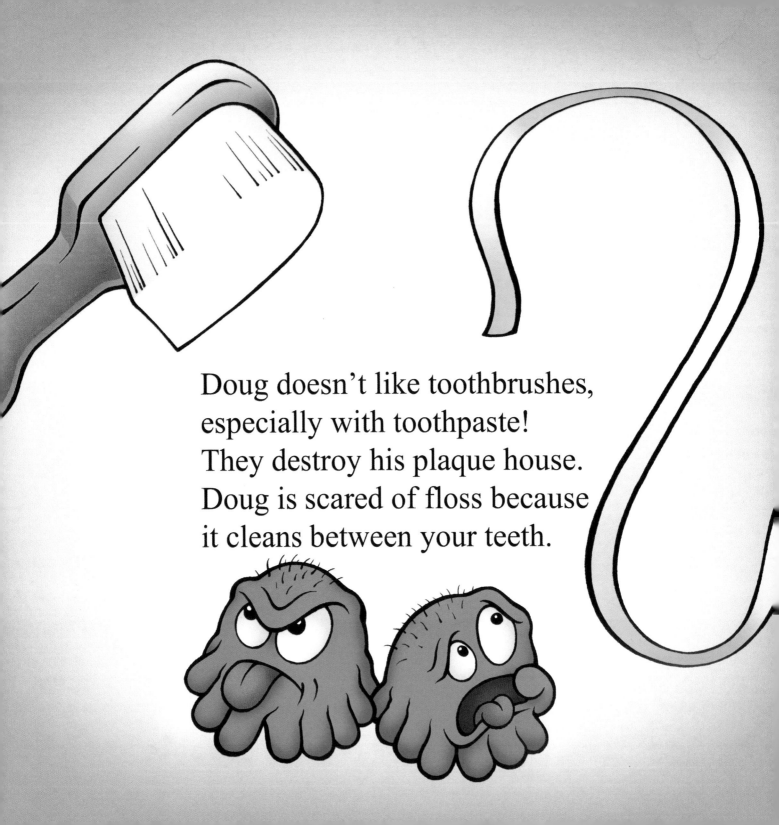

Doug doesn't like toothbrushes, especially with toothpaste! They destroy his plaque house. Doug is scared of floss because it cleans between your teeth.

When a toothbrush cleans your teeth,
Doug and his friends have to run between
your teeth to hide.

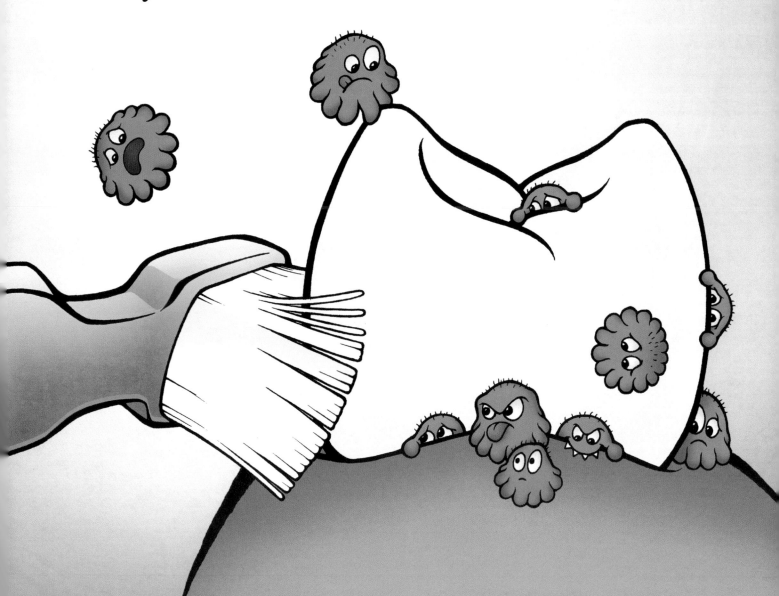

When floss cleans between your teeth,
sugarbugs can't hide there anymore.
They are flossed out of your mouth!

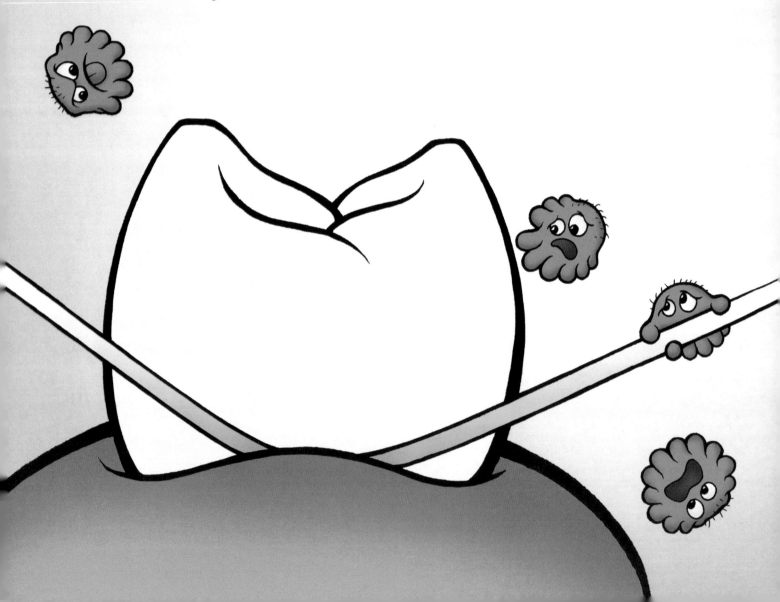

When Doug is flossed out of your mouth, he gets washed down the drain. Say "Goodbye!" to Doug… "We hope to never see you or your friends again!"

So always remember to brush and floss every day to keep sugarbugs out of your mouth forever!

Find out more...

Note to Parents and Teachers: Dental disease is one of the most common and preventable diseases in children and adults. When children are about six years old their permanent teeth will start to come in, and through some very simple steps, they can keep these teeth healthy for their whole life.

This book was written to teach children how, and more importantly, why they need to keep their teeth clean. The following pages are meant to clarify the story and answer any questions that you may have. Feel free to talk to your dental professional to find simple and easy ways to prevent tooth decay and gum disease.

www.sugarbugdoug.com

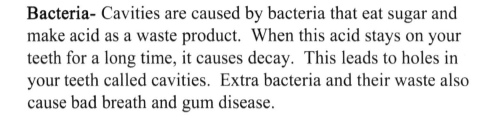

Bacteria- Cavities are caused by bacteria that eat sugar and make acid as a waste product. When this acid stays on your teeth for a long time, it causes decay. This leads to holes in your teeth called cavities. Extra bacteria and their waste also cause bad breath and gum disease.

Choose Healthy Foods- Foods filled with sugar such as candy, soda pop, sports drinks and juice are quickly digested by the bacteria living in your mouth. This produces acid that will attack your teeth. Foods like cookies and caramel can be more dangerous, as the sugar can stick to your teeth. Foods like fresh fruits, vegetables and cheese are much healthier for you. Eating them after sugary foods can prevent cavities by cleaning some of the sugar off of your teeth.

Sugar- More important than how much sugar you eat, is how often you eat sugar and how long it stays on your teeth. This is why snacking on sugary treats is so much worse than eating them at meals. Also, giving a toddler a sippy cup filled with juice or milk can be fine for a half an hour, but it can hurt their teeth if they use it all day or all night.

Carbohydrates- Cookies, crackers, pastries and other foods made mostly from refined white flour can be turned into acid just like sugar. The fact that these foods also tend to stick to your teeth makes them more dangerous, leading to plaque build-up and cavities. Breads made from whole grains and fiber are not as easily digested by bacteria, nor do they stick to your teeth as much, making them much healthier for you and your teeth.

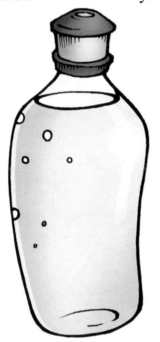

Drink Water- Water helps to wash sugar and acid out of your mouth whenever you drink it. Drinking water after eating is one of the simplest ways to help prevent cavities.

Sugarless Gum- Chewing sugarless gum after meals cleans your teeth and neutralizes the acidic waste that causes cavities and bad breath. Most types of sugarless gum also have sweeteners like "xylitol" that protect your teeth by destroying the bacteria that cause cavities.

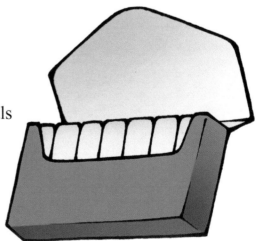

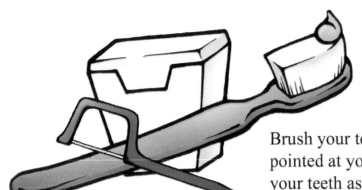

Brush and Floss- Cleaning your teeth at least twice a day is the best way to prevent cavities. The best times to clean your teeth are after meals and before bed.

Brush your teeth using a soft toothbrush with soft circles pointed at your gum line. Be sure to brush all sides of your teeth as well as the top of your tongue.

Floss your teeth- As you floss your teeth, pull the floss toward each tooth, then push against the other tooth. Work the floss up and down gently, between each of your teeth and behind your last tooth on each side.

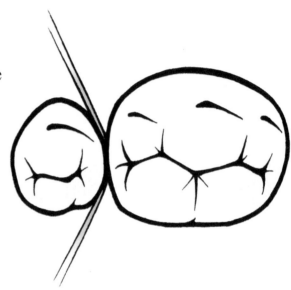

Nighttime- The time that you sleep is the longest that your teeth can be clean, and if they are dirty, it is one of the most dangerous times. Food and bacteria that are in your mouth when you are asleep are not rinsed away or swallowed as often as when you are awake. These extra bacteria and their waste are also one of the main causes of morning breath.

Fluoride- Using a fluoride mouthwash after brushing and flossing will make your teeth much stronger against the acid that bacteria make. It can even heal small cavities that you may have. As good as fluoride is for your teeth, you should never swallow mouthwash or toothpaste. Whenever you rinse your mouth with fluoride, do not eat or drink for at least a half hour. This allows fluoride the time it needs to soak into your teeth to make them strong.

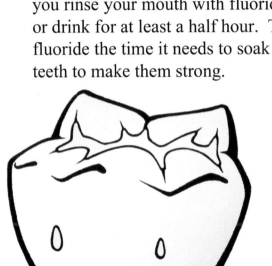

Sealants- Most back teeth have grooves that are very difficult to clean. Bacteria can hide there and start cavities fairly easily. Having a dentist glue a small amount of white plastic to your teeth will make it much harder for bacteria to start cavities there. This white plastic is called a "sealant," and can be done without drilling or shots.

Sensitive gums- If you are just starting to keep your teeth clean, and you have a lot of plaque and calculus, then your infected gums could be very sensitive to brushing and flossing. This is especially true of flossing. Getting your teeth cleaned by a dentist or hygienist and then keeping your teeth clean will allow your gums to heal so they will not hurt anymore.

Glossary

Acid (**ass**-id) A substance that can dissolve teeth and other materials.

Bacteria (bak-**tihr**-ee-uh) Tiny creatures that live everywhere and can only be seen with a microscope. Germs.

Calculus (**kal**-kyuh-luss) A yellow/brown substance that forms on teeth. It is made up of food, calcium, bacteria and their waste. Calcified plaque. The same as tartar.

Cavity (**kav**-uh-tee) A hole that forms in a tooth as it is dissolved by acid. Tooth decay.

Floss (**floss**) A thin strand of thread used to clean between teeth.

Fluoride (flor-**id**) A chemical added to toothpaste and mouthwash that makes teeth strong and acid resistant.

Gums (**guhms**) The "skin" inside your mouth that protects your teeth and covers your jaw.

Plaque (**plak**) A film of sticky material that forms on your teeth made up of food, bacteria and their waste products. Biofilm.

Sealant (**seel**-ant) A plastic filling placed on teeth to prevent decay.

Sugar (**shug**- ur) Sweeteners in foods that bacteria thrive on. When bacteria eat sugar they make acid that will attack your teeth.

Tartar (**tar**-tur) The same as calculus.

Xylitol (**zye**-luh-tawl) A sweetener that is poisonous to the bacteria that cause tooth decay.
It can be found in "sugarless gum."

Infected vs. Healthy teeth and gums

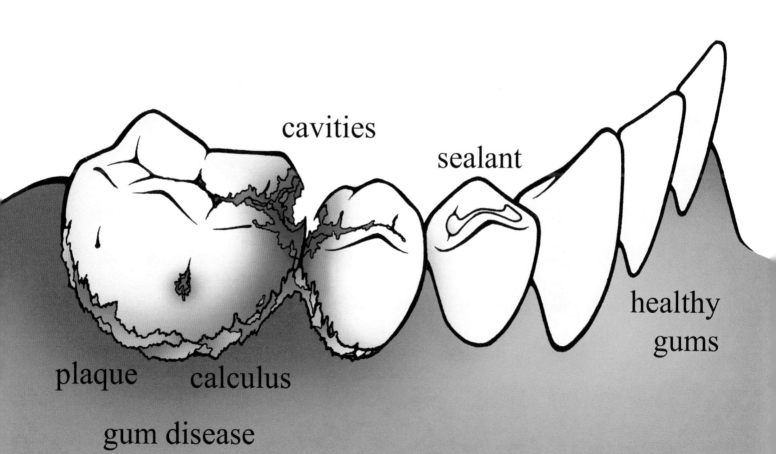

cavities

sealant

healthy gums

plaque

calculus

gum disease

About the Author

Ben Magleby graduated from University of the Pacific School of Dentistry and has enjoyed practicing as a general dentist in North Carolina and California.

Dr. Ben earned his bachelor's degree in art with an emphasis in illustration and sculpture; he enjoys drawing, painting and many other types of art.

Dr. Ben and his wife live in California with their three children.

Made in the USA
Columbia, SC
11 January 2018